RED PLANET

by Moira Butterfield • Illustrated by Jonathan Woodward

To Ian, Jack, and Gus, always ~ **M.B.**

For Mali and Samson, my two creative, nature-loving cubs.
May your world always be full of wonder ~ **J.W.**

360 DEGREES, an imprint of Tiger Tales
5 River Road, Suite 128, Wilton, CT 06897
Published in the United States 2021
Originally published in Great Britain 2020
by Little Tiger Press Ltd.
Text by Moira Butterfield • Illustrations by Jonathan Woodward
Text and illustrations copyright © 2020 Little Tiger Press Ltd.
ISBN-13: 978-1-944530-95-2
ISBN-10: 1-944530-95-9
Printed in China • LT/1800/0154/0421
All rights reserved
2 4 6 8 10 9 7 5 3 1
www.tigertalesbooks.com

The Forest Stewardship Council® (FSC®) is an international,
non-governmental organization dedicated to promoting responsible
management of the world's forests. FSC® operates a system of forest
certification and product labeling that allows consumers to identify wood
and wood-based products from well-managed forests and other sources.

For more information about the FSC®, please visit their website at www.fsc.org

Contents

Our Red Planet

The world's hottest locations are its deserts and volcanoes. They are incredibly dangerous places for humans to go. Reading about them is by far the safest way to explore them!

KEY
Hot deserts
Volcanic regions
· · · Equator

What Is a Desert?

Deserts are dry places with very little rain. They can be super hot or very cold.

North America

The Desert Belt

Most of our deserts are near the equator. The equator is an imaginary line around the middle of the Earth. It receives more of the Sun's energy than other areas.

South America

Around a **third** of Earth's land is covered in desert.

Between **50** and **70** volcanoes erupt each year on Earth.

What Is a Volcano?

A volcano is a place where red-hot molten rock called lava finds its way up to the surface from deep beneath the Earth.

More Hot Spots

Eruptions can create giant lava lakes, steaming-hot water springs, and bubbling mud geysers.

Europe

Asia

Africa

Oceania

Life Finds a Way

Some incredibly tough animals and plants find ways to survive in the world's hottest regions.

Antarctica

Hot Spots

There are some extreme sizzling spots all around the world, where the temperatures can get high enough to melt pavement or cook food without an oven.

Biggest Desert

The world's largest hot desert is the Sahara in North Africa. It's a similar size to all of China or the United States.

The Sahara is often the hottest place on Earth.

Hottest Spot

A place with a fiery name, Furnace Creek, holds the record for the hottest place on Earth, with an air temperature of 134°F (56.6°C). It's in Death Valley, California.

Creatures like roadrunners manage to live here.

Hottest Night

The North African town of Quriyat, in Oman, has broken the record for the hottest "low" temperature. Even in the coolest part of the night, the temperature was a sizzling 108.7°F (42.6°C)!

The heat is enough to melt the roads.

Biggest Volcano

Mauna Loa, in Hawaii, is the world's biggest active volcano. It's even taller than Everest (the world's highest mountain), although part of it is underwater.

Mauna Loa erupts every few years, pumping out red-hot lava.

Largest Hot Spring

Frying Pan Lake in Waimangu, New Zealand, is the world's biggest hot spring. It's a pool of steaming-hot water as big as several soccer fields.

The water is 140°F (60°C), so it's not safe to swim.

Desert Tour

Not all deserts look the same or have similar weather. Some are sandy, some are rocky, and some are actually freezing cold!

A desert is a place that has less than 10 inches (25 cm) of rain each year.

Hottest Deserts

Subtropical deserts are the hottest in the world. They are caused by the way air moves around the world, dropping all of its rain elsewhere. They might be sandy or rocky places.

There's nothing like the
GREAT AUSTRALIAN DESERTS

THE JEWEL OF
Sahara
NORTH AFRICA

Some deserts don't belong in this book. They are icy! The Antarctic is the world's **biggest** desert, but it's freezing.

Nights can be freezing even in the hottest deserts. There has even been **snowfall** at the edge of the Sahara.

Mountain Deserts

Some deserts have little rain because they are in the shadow of mountains. All the rain falls on the mountains and never reaches the desert.

GOBI DESERT

CHINA, MONGOLIA & THE HIMALAYAS

PATAGONIAN DESERT

It will take your breath away!

ARGENTINA & ANDES MOUNTAINS

The center of Chile's Atacama Desert had no rainfall for **500** years.

Namib Desert

Visit Namibia

ATACAMA DESERT

SOUTH AMERICAN TREASURE

Seaside Deserts

Coastal deserts miss out on water because of their position by cold seas. The ocean winds bring them fog instead of rain.

Survivors

Birds and mammals have some clever survival tricks, too. They have many different ways to adapt to the heat.

burrowing owl

elf owl

DIY Burrow Builder

The white-throated woodrat (found in North and Central America) piles up fragments of desert plants and stones into a huge shelter. Underneath are hidden tunnels and rooms for food storing and sleeping.

white-throated woodrat

Shady Shelters

The elf owl hops into old woodpecker holes in trees and giant cacti. Its neighbor, the burrowing owl, uses abandoned burrows dug by prairie dogs to hide from the Sun.

Big Ears

Most desert mammals avoid getting too hot in the desert by coming out only at night or in the early morning. Saharan fennec foxes have extra-big ears to help them, too. These act like radiators, letting out heat from the body.

Cool Skills

American black vultures and Australian kangaroos both have unusual ways of cooling themselves down. The vultures pee and poop on their own legs, while the kangaroos lick their forearms to coat them in cooling spit.

Water Carrier

The male sandgrouse has a special way to get water to his chicks in the bone-dry deserts of Africa and Asia. He flies to the nearest waterhole and uses his tummy feathers like a sponge to soak up the water. When he returns, his chicks use their bills to squeeze the water out.

fennec fox

kangaroo

male sandgrouse

Desert Dinner

Some desert birds get all the water they need by hunting other creatures. The roadrunner zips around American deserts at high speed, gobbling up lizards and snakes.

roadrunner

Realm of the Reptile

Reptiles need to absorb heat to stay alive, so warm places are a good location for them. It's hard for any creature to survive in extreme heat. But some Sun-loving reptiles have smart ways of coping.

Desert Dancing

The shovel-snouted lizard has to cope with searing African heat in the Namib Desert. When the ground starts to overheat, it does a kind of hopping dance, lifting its feet to keep them cool. It can dive beneath the sand, too.

shovel-snouted
lizard

water-holding
frog

Sand Swimmers

Some small lizards can "swim" through sand by moving just beneath the surface. They have narrow heads and smooth, shiny scales to help them slip through the grains. There's even a sand-swimming lizard called a sandfish, which lives in the Sahara.

sandfish

Water Keeper

The water-holding frog lives in southern Australia, which can be hot and dry for months. It can store enough water in its bladder and skin pockets to live for five years without needing to drink.

Staying Chilled

The desert tortoise, found in the southwestern United States and Mexico, spends most of its time in cool, cozy burrows. It can stay resting for months, living off fat and liquid stored in its body, and will only crawl out when the temperature outside is comfortable.

desert tortoise

Hot Mover

Desert sand can get dangerously hot, but the sidewinder rattlesnake protects itself from getting scorched by wriggling sideways very fast. It hardly touches the ground as it speeds along, and as soon as it stops, it quickly buries itself beneath the sand.

sidewinder rattlesnake

West African crocodile

Desert Surprise

You might not expect crocodiles to live in the desert, but the West African crocodile does. It rests in caves or burrows during the dry season and slithers out to the nearest waterhole when the rains come.

Tiny but Tough

Desert insects have some very clever ways of surviving in their scorching-hot desert homes.

Plant Juice Bar

Many desert insects get all the water they need from munching on plants. The milkweed bug gets its name from the sticky white juice it drinks from the milkweed plant, found in deserts in the United States.

milkweed bug

Scorched Sand

The African Namib Desert hardly ever gets rain, but fog sometimes rolls over it from the nearby ocean.

darkling beetle

Fog Catcher

A local type of darkling beetle has a clever way of catching fog to drink. The back of the beetle is covered in tiny bumps. When it's foggy, it stands with its bottom in the air. Droplets of fog settle on the bumps and run down into the beetle's mouth. This is called "fog basking."

Digging Down

Many desert insects hide during the blazing daytime heat. Desert crickets use their stout, spiny legs to dig underground burrows, where they can shelter.

desert cricket

Hunting and Hiding

Tiny hunters, like scorpions and spiders, get almost all the moisture they need from a juicy meal. So they spend their time lurking among rocks and sand dunes, ready to pounce!

desert hairy scorpion

Silver Secret

Saharan silver ants are able to come out to look for food in the heat of the day, when most other insects have to hide. Their backs and sides are covered in silver hairs that reflect sunlight away.

Saharan silver ant

Plant Superstars

The cacti family are the top plant survival experts. They are found in the baking-hot deserts of North and South America.

Secrets of the Cacti

- When it rains, the inside of a cactus stores water like a wet sponge.

- Cactus roots spread out near the surface so they can quickly soak up any rain.

- Cacti don't lose water through their leaves like other plants do because they have no leaves! Their waxy, thick outer skin helps them keep water in, too.

- Cacti often have ridges that look like pleats. They can stretch out like a fan when the cactus swells up with water.

prickly pear

Don't Drink Me

It's a myth that people can drink water safely from a cactus—it's likely to give you a bad stomachache. You can eat some types of cacti fruit, though, if you can pick them without getting pricked!

pencil cholla

California barrel

Keep Off!

The teddy bear cholla cactus isn't as cuddly as it sounds. It has some of the sharpest spines of all cacti, and they are hooked, too, so they're hard to remove. Another lethally spiky cactus goes by the nickname "horse crippler" because it grows low to the ground. Its spikes are almost as long as fingers!

teddy bear cholla

horse crippler

silver cholla

scarlet hedgehog

Don't Eat Me

With so little food available, many desert animals would like to eat cacti. But their sharp thorns and tough skin keep hungry visitors away.

Water Champions

The cacti water-storing champion is the giant saguaro, which can grow as tall as a four-story building. After heavy rainfall, large saguaros can store enough water to fill three bathtubs.

saguaro

organ pipe

Rainy Desert Days

Many surprises appear when it rains in a super-hot, dry location!

Slithering Shrimp

shield shrimp

A strange creature called a shield shrimp hatches and slithers from the mud when it rains in the Australian desert. Its eggs can lie dormant underground for up to seven years.

spadefoot toad

Lazy Toad

Desert toads and frogs sometimes burrow below the ground, where they stay hidden for months waiting for rain. Then they all hop out to mate and lay eggs. American spadefoot toads can stay hidden underground for up to a decade!

Superseeds

Desert plant seeds can lie resting for years before conditions are right for them to sprout. The record-breaker is a 2,000-year-old date palm seed found in Masada, Israel. Scientists found out how old it was, then managed to make it grow.

date palm tree

The Big Bloom

Seeds that have been lying in the desert soil suddenly grow when enough rain falls. They carpet the ground in a beautiful show of flowers called a super bloom.

monarch butterfly

ocotillo

Animal Helpers

Animals help to pollinate the desert flowers when they arrive to gather nectar. The pollen rubs onto them, and they take it to the next flower they visit. Creatures also help to spread desert seeds by eating cactus fruit and then dropping the seeds out when they poop!

rufous hummingbird

chuparosa

morning glory

Heat from Below

The Earth doesn't get all of its heat from the Sun. Some of it comes up from deep below the surface, where temperatures are so high that even rock melts.

Baby Volcano

A volcano forms when magma—which is mostly made from melted rock—fills up a giant chamber below the ground. Pressure from underneath pushes the magma upward, until it erupts out of the ground as red-hot lava.

Hill of Heat

Over time, lava builds up to form a hill shape with a crater in the middle. This is the shape we recognize as a volcano. Sometimes the lava also comes out through side exits called dikes. Ash, poisonous gas, and lumps of rock called volcanic bombs can also shoot out during an eruption.

crater

dike

lava

magma

The **hottest** lava measured so far was from the Kīlauea volcano in Hawaii. It was **2,138°F (1170°C)**.

magma chamber

Volcano Shapes

A volcano's shape depends on the type of eruption that created it, and the sort of material that came out during the eruption.

Composite cone volcanoes look like cone-shaped mountains. They are made when lava and ash are layered up over many eruptions.

Shield volcanoes are shaped like upturned saucers. They are created by very runny lava that spreads out, rather than piling up.

Cinder cone volcanoes are high, with steep slopes. They are caused when a very explosive eruption piles up material around one single hole.

Inside Earth

Beneath the Earth's crust is a thick layer of molten rock called the mantle.

The core of the Earth has two layers—an outer core of liquid metal and a solid metal inner core.

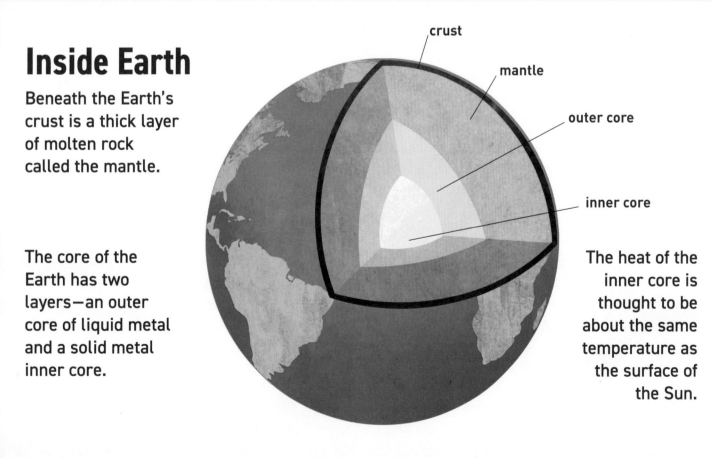

crust

mantle

outer core

inner core

The heat of the inner core is thought to be about the same temperature as the surface of the Sun.

Steamy Spots

When heat escapes from cracks in the Earth's surface, it often brings with it hot springs, shooting steam, and bubbly mud.

Old Faithful

Hot springs that send boiling water and steam spurting up into the air are called geysers. Yellowstone Park in the United States has many of the world's geysers, including a world-famous one nicknamed Old Faithful. It spouts boiling water and scorching steam roughly 20 times a day.

Old Faithful spurts up to **138 feet (42 m)** high. That's about as tall as a nine-story building!

Lava Lakes

Sometimes volcano craters are so wide they are called lava lakes. The world's largest is in the Democratic Republic of Congo in Africa. It's on Mount Nyiragongo, in a crater 820 feet (250 m) across, which is as wide as 10 Olympic swimming pools.

Monkey Spa

Japan's Jōshin'etsu-kōgen National Park is cold and snowy for part of the year, but the macaque monkeys who live there stay warm by bathing in its hot, steamy volcanic springs.

It's possible to swim in some hot springs, but others are so hot they are **deadly!**

macaque monkey

Mud Volcanoes

Sometimes heated water mixes with earth, and bubbles up as a mud volcano.

Volcano Life

Erupting volcanoes destroy the habitats around them, but incredible as it sounds, some creatures do manage to live in these super-scorched surroundings.

hammerhead shark

Welcome to Sharkcano

A giant underwater volcano called Kavachi sits in the Pacific near the Solomon Islands. The water in its crater is hot and full of acid chemicals, so scientists were amazed when they sent a robot submarine down and found hammerhead sharks and other marine life surrounding the volcano.

Lava Crickets

Hawaiian lava crickets love living on new volcano lava. They turn up as soon as it starts cooling. They eat dead plant fragments and sea foam. Once the land around the eruption has fully cooled and starts to recover, the crickets leave. They prefer it hot and tough!

lava cricket

Lava to Jungle

Even after the earth is scorched and plants destroyed, life gradually comes back after a volcano eruption. It just takes a little time.

1 After three or four years, small plants such as ferns and algae return. Birds drop plant seeds in their poop as they fly overhead, or seeds get blown in on the wind. Insects then visit, too.

2 Gradually, dead plants and insects rot down, creating soil. Around 10 years after an eruption, the first grasses and trees appear.

3 Over a few decades, as more and more soil gets made, the sides of the volcano might even grow a thick jungle or forest.

Hot-water Life

There are many volcanoes and geysers underwater. The geysers are called hydrothermal vents.

Geyser Chimneys

Volcanic heat from inside the Earth shoots hot water up from the seabed. This creates a hydrothermal vent. Sometimes rock particles, called minerals, build up to create chimney shapes around the vent.

Hydrothermal vent chimneys can grow up to **180 feet (54.8 m)** tall. That's as tall as the Leaning Tower of Pisa!

Black or White

Some of the chimneys are called black smokers because they belch out dark-colored chemicals. Some are white smokers, shooting out pale-colored material.

Robot submarines are able to film hydrothermal vents, which are found very deep in the ocean.

Kiwa crab

chimney

Extreme Life

Tiny bacteria gather around the hydrothermal vents, living off the chemicals in the water. They are called extremophiles because they can survive in extremely hot temperatures.

Making Food

Extremophiles feed on the chemicals from the vent and turn them into different chemicals in their bodies. This makes them a tasty meal for bigger animals, like tube worms, shrimps, and crabs.

Giant Worms

A tube worm doesn't have a mouth. It soaks up food from the water through its skin. Some tube worms can grow as tall as a human adult.

Eel City

Hundreds of deep-sea eels have been found living around a hydrothermal vent near Samoa in the Pacific. There are so many there that scientists have nicknamed it Eel City.

eel

tube worm

eyeless shrimp

zoarcid fish

Homes in the Heat

If you lived in one of the world's hottest locations, you'd need to find a way to stay cool. These homes are built to help shield the hot Sun.

Desert Tent

The sides of this Bedouin goat-hair tent are propped open during the day to keep it cool. At night, it can be closed to make it warm and cozy. Tents like this are traditionally used in North African deserts.

White Walls

Buildings painted white stay cooler than dark buildings because the white color reflects the Sun's heat away from the walls. White-painted homes are popular in desert areas around the world.

Breeze Catchers

Middle Eastern homes in Iran and Dubai sometimes have wind towers on the roof to keep them cool. The towers, called barjeel, funnel the breeze down into the rooms below.

Cave Homes

A cave is a cool, shady place to live. There are many houses built into caves in hot spots around the world, including almost all of the homes in the Australian town of Coober Pedy. Summers are baking hot there.

Red-hot SOS

The world is getting warmer because pollution in the air is trapping the Sun's heat around the planet. It's likely that more locations will become super hot and very dry, making it hard for creatures and plants to survive. But there are ways to cut down on pollution and slow down global warming.

Clean Power

Burning coal or oil in a power plant is a common way to make electricity, but it puts pollution into the air. Wind power and solar power are much cleaner ways to create energy. Wind turbines and solar panels on rooftops help power homes more cleanly.

wind turbine

solar panels

Clean Engines

electric car

Engines that burn fuel put pollution into the air, but electric cars are much cleaner. Airplanes cause a lot of pollution. Maybe one day, they will partly run on electric batteries instead of jet engines.

charging station

We Can Help

We all need to do our best to stop polluting the world. Why not start today?

Champion Recycler

It takes energy to make everything we use, so it's a good idea to use less. Recycle boxes, bags, bottles, and containers, and get your family to join in.

Save Energy

Turn off lights or computers when you don't need them, and save energy on heating by shutting doors and putting on a sweater.

Muscle Power

Start walking and biking to save on car trips. You'll be helping to cut down pollution, and you'll be keeping fit, too!

The world is an extraordinary and precious place, but it needs our help to keep it from getting hotter. Let's do all we can!

Animal & Plant Index